D1442648

WELCOME TO THE WORLD OF ANIMALS

Frogs and Toads

Diane Swanson

Gareth Stevens Publishing
A WORLD ALMANAC EDUCATION GROUP COMPANY

Please visit our web site at: www.garethstevens.com
For a free color catalog describing Gareth Stevens Publishing's list of high-quality books
and multimedia programs, call 1-800-542-2595 (USA) or 1-800-387-3178 (Canada).
Gareth Stevens Publishing's fax: (414) 332-3567.

The publishers acknowledge the support of the Canada Council for the Arts and the Cultural Services
Branch of the Government of British Columbia in making this publication possible.

Library of Congress Cataloging-in-Publication Data

Swanson, Diane, 1944-
    Frogs and toads / by Diane Swanson.
      p. cm. — (Welcome to the world of animals)
    Includes index.
    Summary: An introduction to the physical characteristics, behaviors, and habitat of frogs and
toads.
    ISBN 0-8368-4023-2 (lib. bdg.)
    1. Frogs—Juvenile literature. 2. Toads—Juvenile literature. [1. Frogs. 2. Toads.] I. Title.
QL668.E2S93 2004
597.8—dc22   2003061254

This edition first published in 2004 by
Gareth Stevens Publishing
A World Almanac Education Group Company
330 West Olive Street, Suite 100
Milwaukee, WI 53212 USA

This U.S. edition © 2004 by Gareth Stevens, Inc. Original edition © 2002 by Diane Swanson.
First published in 2002 by Whitecap Books, Vancouver. Additional end matter © 2004
by Gareth Stevens, Inc.

Series editor: Betsy Rasmussen
Design: Melissa Valuch
Cover design: Steve Penner

Cover photograph: John Mielcarek/Dembinsky Photo Assoc.
Photo credits: Skip Moody/Dembinsky Photo Assoc. 4, 6, 22; Rob and Ann Simpson 8; John
Mielcarek/Dembinsky Photo Assoc. 10, 16, 20; Kitchin & Hurst 12, 14; Gary Meszaros/Dembinsky Photo
Assoc. 18; Jens Vindum/California Academy of Sciences 24; Photo on 26 courtesy of ACO Polymer
Products, Inc.; Wayne Lynch 28, 30

Printed in the United States of America

1 2 3 4 5 6 7 8 9 08 07 06 05 04

Contents

World of Difference

Whether warty or smooth, dry or moist — there is little real difference between the croaking critters folks call toads and those called frogs. To scientists, they are all just frogs that have adapted to different kinds of homes.

Frogs and toads are amphibians: animals that spend part of their lives in water and part on land. While other amphibians — such as salamanders and newts — have tails, adult frogs and toads do not.

There are about thirty-five hundred kinds of frogs and toads in the world, but they do not all live in North America.

Like other frogs and toads, the American toad oozes toxins from its skin.

A gray tree frog blends well with the fungus it sits on.

Canada and the United States are home to about one hundred different kinds. With its warmer climate, Mexico has even more.

The grass frog is one of the smallest in North America and the world. It is only about the size of your thumbnail. At the other extreme are bullfrogs that can measure 8 inches (20 centimeters) from end to end.

Frogs and toads come in several colors, including brown, black, green, yellow, and white. Many can hide by blending in with what is around them. A brown tree frog called a spring peeper, for example, is hard to spot among dead leaves.

Shifts in light, moisture, and temperature can cause frogs and toads to vary their colors. A little Pacific tree frog might change from green to gray to yellow and back to green again — all within eight minutes.

FABULOUS FROGS, TERRIFIC TOADS

Here are some things frogs and toads can do.

- Just by sitting on damp soil, a spadefoot toad can absorb water through its skin.

- Lightweight tree frogs can walk upside down — even on smooth surfaces.

- Over the summer, a single toad can eat as many as ten thousand insects.

- Sucked up by hurricanes, little frogs sometimes travel long distances before falling like rain.

Where in the World

In the grass, beneath a rock, under the water, or up a tree — frogs and toads are almost everywhere and on every continent, except Antarctica. Most are found in hot, humid countries, but wood frogs live farther north than the Arctic Circle!

Different kinds of frogs and toads adopt different kinds of homes, including damp forests, dry deserts, cold mountain streams, and city gardens. Some spend much of their time in water. Others live mostly on land — up in trees, in bushes, or even underground.

Body temperatures of frogs and toads change with their surroundings. Some dig

A good burrower, this spadefoot toad peeks out of its little hole.

9

The large eardrum behind the eye of the bullfrog is easy to spot.

burrows or bury themselves in sand or mud to cool down and avoid drying out. In Mexico and southern Texas, the Mexican burrowing toad spends a lot of its life beneath the surface. Like most tunneling frogs and toads, it digs in backward, scraping and scooping with knobs on its hind feet.

In places with cold winters, many frogs bury themselves in the bottom of ponds and small lakes. They live on fat stored in their bodies and take in oxygen from the water through their skin. They sleep deeply for months — this is called hibernation.

Day to day, frogs and toads do not usually travel far. Many hunt for food inside their own territories. Then they head back to shelter, often settling under stones and logs.

ALIEN HOPPERS

Capture frogs and toads from one pond and release them in another? BAD idea! Adding new kinds of frogs and toads to any pond causes trouble.

Bullfrogs from eastern North America were taken to western North America and raised as food for people. When these aliens moved into an area, they soon spread out on their own. The bullfrogs have been eating up small western frogs, such as red-legged frogs, as well as fish, snakes, and birds ever since.

11

World in Motion

Having no tails helps frogs and toads jump by making it easier to kick off with both back legs at once. Frogs and toads with narrow bodies and long legs usually leap the farthest. Those with wide bodies and short legs often just hop or walk.

In water, the animals can swim fast by kicking their back legs much as they do when they are jumping on land. They spread out their webbed back feet to push their bodies forward, and they press their front legs tightly against their sides.

Instead of swimming, warty northern cricket frogs and a few others sometimes skip across a pond. With a series of quick

Up, off, and away! A bullfrog makes a mighty leap.

13

It is easy for a Pacific tree frog to squat safely on a skinny stem.

jumps, they can bounce along the surface.

Little tree frogs get around mostly by climbing — grabbing onto twigs or branches. To escape danger from enemies such as snakes and birds, they usually jump. And they are good at it! Large sticky pads on their toes help them hang onto almost everything.

Some also have a sticky webbing between their toes. These frogs can cling to surfaces as steep and smooth as windows and doors.

Balancing on slender twigs is no problem for tree frogs. Their slightly flattened bodies make it possible for them to spread their weight out evenly. They also press their loose belly skin snugly against any surface, which helps to hold them in place.

L-O-N-G JUMPS

Ready, set . . . leap. Every year, there is a special event — the Jumping Frog Jubilee — held in Angels Camp, California.

To enter, frogs must be at least 4 inches (10 centimeters) long. Each one makes three jumps, then judges measure the total straight-line distance to its final landing spot.

A bullfrog named Rosie the Ribiter holds the unbroken record. In 1986, she covered a distance greater than the length of three beds placed end to end.

15

World Full of Food

Flies, ants, slugs, and worms are all yummy meals for frogs and toads! Frogs and toads dine on what is handy and small enough to fit into their mouths. Big croakers also feast on mice, small snakes, fish, and even other frogs and toads. Some catch bats that swoop to the water at night to drink.

It is lucky that frogs and toads are not fussy eaters. Stuck in a basement or garage, toads easily change their menu from worms and butterflies to spiders and centipedes.

Frogs that spend much of their lives in water can hide and hunt at the same time. Their big eyes and nostrils usually sit on the

Thick, green duckweed makes a great cover for a hungry green frog.

Chomp! A leopard frog captures a dragonfly for lunch.

tops of their heads, so frogs can see and breathe while keeping mostly out of sight. There is a hitch, though. The frogs cannot spot what is right in front of them. For that, they have to turn sideways.

A long tongue serves most frogs and toads well. It is normally attached to the front of the mouth, so it can zoom out far to catch dinner. The food sticks to the gooey tip and is drawn in as the tongue returns to the mouth. The whole action is very fast. One high-speed camera filmed a toad's tongue as it shot out, nabbed a worm, and returned — all in less than .07 second.

Catching food is harder work for the tailed frog of North America's mountain streams. Its tongue is attached to the back — not the front — of its mouth, so the frog has to catch insects by snapping them up.

BIG GULP!

Now you see it. Now you don't. Whatever frogs and toads catch for lunch is normally swallowed whole.

To get the food down, a meal might take two or three gulps — plus some help from the critter's eyeballs.

Muscles pull on one or both of the eyes, pressing them down hard against the roof of the mouth. That forces the food back and into the animal's throat. No wonder frogs and toads blink wildly as they swallow.

19

World of Words

Most frogs and toads are built to sing. Besides their strong voice boxes, large stretchy vocal sacs help them make sounds. The singing ranges from warbles to whistles to croaks to chuckles. Some of the songs are short, while others can last for several minutes.

Each kind of frog and toad makes its own special type of music. Cricket frogs click. Chorus frogs rattle. Mexican tree frogs sputter. Wood frogs quack. The smaller animals usually produce high-pitched tones, while large ones often have deep-pitched voices. But when it comes to

A singing spring peeper inflates its see-through vocal sac.

volume, even little frogs and toads can make a lot of noise. The shrill singing of a spring peeper can be heard one-half mile (.8 kilometer) away — and sometimes all night long!

Many kinds of male frogs and toads sing to attract mates at breeding times. They crowd together and croon. The females depend on these songs — more than sight or smell — to find males ready to mate.

When it is time to mate, green frogs gather together.

Male frogs and toads might sing to warn other males to go away. Their singing might also interrupt the mating songs of their competition.

Grabbed by an enemy, such as a hungry heron or raccoon, frogs and toads might scream. The noise does not act as a warning to others, but it can shock the enemy into letting its victim go. Still, there are moments when it is best to say nothing and simply play dead. Animals hunting for live food ignore these frogs and toads.

SORTING THE SONGS

It was a warm spring night as a female bullfrog arrived at the edge of a pond. The voices of many different frogs and toads were already filling the air. Green frogs were plinking and plunking. Spring peepers were whistling, and American toads were trilling for ten seconds at a time.

The bullfrog waited, listening closely for just one song. Suddenly, she heard "Jug o'rum. Jug o'rum." And with that, she was off to find the singer — her mate.

World of Mates

Mating frogs and toads often go where there is water. They gather by the hundreds — or thousands — at ponds, shallow lakes, swamps, drainage ditches, even puddles. Some find their way to the same spot year after year, using smells, sights, and sounds to guide them.

Changes in light, temperature, and moisture help signal the start of breeding seasons. And for many frogs and toads, that means springtime. Breeding seasons are long for some, short for others. Bullfrogs, for instance, have several months each year to mate, while wood frogs in the north might have only a day or two.

The tailed frog has no true tail, but its tail-like part helps it mate.

25

For small animals, using a "toad tunnel" is the safest way to cross a road.

Female frogs and toads often respond to the songs of the males, who usually call out from good egg-laying places. But some males sit in silence. Then they try to grab females as they head toward the singing males.

Oddly, male tailed frogs have no voices at all. They have to find their mates by swimming silently over riverbeds. Male western toads can produce sounds, but they cannot all make breeding calls. Instead, they might hunt for mates day and night, grabbing whatever seems like a female toad — even a thick twig in the water.

When most frogs and toads mate, the male grasps the female tightly with his front legs. As soon as she lays her eggs, he fertilizes them. If a male clutches a female who has released her eggs, she makes a special sound that tells him she has already mated.

TOAD TUNNELS

Toads crossing busy highways to reach mating ponds risk getting killed. Many travel in such large groups that a single car can strike down dozens at a time.

People in parts of North America created tunnels beneath some high-traffic roads along toad routes.

They built low fences to guide the critters toward the entrances. The tunnels have almost completely eliminated toad road deaths in their areas.

New World

Eggs in clumps, eggs in strings, and a few frogs lay their eggs in foam. By kicking their legs, white-lipped frogs in Texas and Mexico whip mucus and water into a stiff froth, or foam. This bubbly nest protects the eggs from getting too hot or drying out.

Depending on which kinds of frogs or toads they are, the females might lay only a few eggs or several thousand! Hatching times also vary, but one day, young frogs and toads — called tadpoles — emerge from the eggs. They seldom look anything like their parents. They do not even have legs. Instead, the tadpoles have long, strong tails

Wood frog tadpoles will hatch out of this clump of eggs.

A muddy puddle can be home to spadefoot toad tadpoles.

that help them swim. Like fish, they breathe with gills, not lungs.

Hungry tadpoles eat just about any plants and bacteria they can. They might also dine on animals that have died in the water. For feeding in swift streams, tailed frog tadpoles have big suckers that help them stay in place.

As tadpoles grow, their bodies change. Their tails and gills disappear, and they develop legs and lungs. They begin to look like adult frogs and toads, and soon they are ready to leave the water. Many kinds of tadpoles become adults a few months after they hatch. Some kinds take only days, while others take years.

Throughout their lives, toads and frogs struggle to escape enemies, such as newts, crows, and skunks. They do not usually live long, but bullfrogs can live to be fifteen or twenty years old.

TADPOLE-EATING TADPOLES

Spadefoot toad tadpoles, which often hatch in rain puddles, sometimes feed on their brothers and sisters! Although most of these tadpoles gobble up bits of plants in the water, others become meat eaters.

The tadpoles grow quickly — but not always quickly enough. If a puddle is drying up faster than the plant eaters are maturing, the meat-eating tadpoles devour them, developing even more rapidly. It is all just a matter of survival!

31

Glossary

aliens — animals not naturally found in an area; they are brought into the area from somewhere else.

amphibians — a group of animals that uses gills to breathe when in water as youngsters and lungs to breathe air as adults.

breeding — the mating of animals to produce young.

climate — area weather conditions.

gills — the body parts of a tadpole or a fish used to take oxygen from the water.

hibernation — spending the winter in a deep sleep.

lungs — organs used by animals to breathe air.

mates — pairs of male and female animals that produce young.

mucus — a slimy, protective substance produced by the body.

toxins — poisons produced by an animal or plant.

warty — a bumpiness or knobbiness of the skin.

Index